© 2021 George Beamer
All rights reserved.
ISBN: 9798483764717
ISBN
Library of Congress Control Number: **XXXXX (If applicable)**
LCCN Imprint Name: **City and State (If applicable)**

This book is dedicated to
All of us who believe America is worth saving.

Contents

Forward..5

Introduction 6

Part 1: Definition and Tenets 8

    What is CRT..8

        A Rat by any other Name is still a Rat   10

    The Tenets of CRT 11

        CRT is a Movement/Religion   11

        Race is the Primary Characteristic of a Human   14

        Critical/Correct Think vs. White/Wrong Think   15

        CRT has 2 Objectives 17

Part 2: What we can do about it 21

    This is not a fight, we are all Americans..................21

    Reject CRT wherever you encounter it 22

    We must stop the indoctrination of our children ...25

    Do not Pay for the Revolution 27

    Engage your Representatives 27

Forward

CRT wants to separate and pit us against each other based on labels, lies and the "reframing" of facts, science and history.

CRT They[1] are trying to divide us. Actually, CRT They have already mostly succeeded. We are now in the 3rd generation of indoctrination and the CRT They have pushed their agenda all the way down into our pre-schools.

We have already seen the beginnings of their "revolution" with their "mostly peaceful protests" looting and burning cities across America.

If CRT is allowed to flourish it is the end of America.

It is the end of our freedom. It is the end of the West.

We can choose:

CRT, hate and a culture/race war
-or-
Freedom, love and finding a way to move forward together, as one people

---

[1] "CRT They". When I use this term I mean CRT proponents, advocates, indoctrinators, and allies.

Introduction

This booklet explains what Critical Race Theory (CRT) is, why it's bad and provides some suggestions for what we can do to prevent it from destroying our country (your country).

I have made this booklet as brief and concise as possible in an attempt to maximize the accessibility of the info and hopefully provide some clarity on the amorphous, intentionally confusing topic of CRT.

This booklet is broken into 2 parts:

Part1: CRT, what is it and why it is bad

Part 2: What we can do about it

Disclaimer & Waiver

By continuing to read this booklet you understand and agree to the following:

1. I am simply providing a perspective on a topic for entertainment purposes only and any similarity between that perspective, characterizations, messages or meanings and reality are strictly accidental/unintentional or dumb luck

2. You do NOT have the right to be offended, sorry that is CRT They's rules. If you chronically take offense at everything you probably should skip this booklet

By having read and understood the previous statements and by continuing to read this booklet, you, your family and agents agree to hold me, my past, present, and future friends, family, and business associates harmless and waive all of your rights to any and all legal recourse (except where explicitly prohibited by Federal law or the laws of the state of Ohio).

In short, I and all those folks previously mentioned assume no liability for anything that you may ever do to yourself now or in the future, and you agree that you, your family and agents will never try to blame me or my folks for anything you ever have done, do or will do.

By continuing to read this book you agree that you have read, understood, and agree to the Disclaimer and Waiver above.

These are weird, but crazy is crazy so disclaimers for all☺

Part 1: Definition and Tenets

What is CRT

One of the things that I have seen over and over again when it comes to people discussing CRT, is folks, whether they are parents, content creators, or news casters repeating something like "I don't understand".

Well that is by design, CRT is obtuse, academia nonsense by design. It is Word Warfare meant to confuse, confound and intimidate.

So let's start with a definition:

"Critical race theory (CRT) is a body of legal scholarship and an academic movement of US civil-rights scholars and activists who seek to critically examine the intersection of race and U.S. law and to challenge mainstream American liberal approaches to racial justice. CRT examines social, cultural, and legal issues primarily as they relate to race and racism in the US."[2]

Now that doesn't sound all that insidious but whether or not CRT has been hijacked by its "activists" really isn't the point.

The CRT They have not stopped at a "critical examination of the intersection of race and U.S. law".

---

[2] Wikipedia

They have not condemned the violence and mayhem that has been carried out in their name.

They have leaned into advancing the "movement's" ultimate goal of the destruction of White. In short, the destruction of capitalism, freedom, America and the West.

So just how entrenched is CRT?
It started among law academics in the late 1970's, spread throughout universities by the mid to late 1990's, and has been infecting our K-12 institutions since the early 2000's.

Basically the CRT They own the last 2½ generations of Americans starting with the Millennials.

Because of this, CRT owns most tech companies and most of the mainstream media.

The CRT They controls how we communicate and ultimately what gets communicated.

A Rat by any other Name is still a Rat

Whether it is White Fragility, White Guilt, Wokism, BLM, or ANTIFA, it all comes from and is supported by CRT.

These mini-movements run the spectrum from promoting self loathing[3] and learned helplessness[4] all the way to advocating and engaging in violence against non-believers and law and order.

---

[3] If you are born white you are an oppressor and a racist and you are irredeemable.

[4] If you are born black you are oppressed and a victim and will never be free of oppression.

The Tenets of CRT

CRT is a Movement/Religion
Any time the CRT They claims that CRT is a "set of ideals, not a movement" they are lying. The title of the CRT bible is, "*Critical Race Theory: The Key Writings that Formed the **Movement**".*

CRT They created Intersectionality
CRT They could not destroy the West on their own. They needed allies and with their belief in 2 races[5] their options were limited. That's where Intersectionality comes in.

What's Intersectionality?
Intersectionality is an analytical framework for understanding how aspects of a person's social and political identities combine to create different modes of discrimination and privilege. The term was conceptualized and coined by Kimberlé Williams Crenshaw[6] in a paper in 1989.[7]

Think of it as a social currency. The more groups a person can claim membership in, the more important that person is.

---

[5] More on that later
[6] Note: Kimberlé Williams Crenshaw is one of the founders of CRT
[7] Wikipedia

Note that all the categories or groups claim to be oppressed and white straight men are not allowed in any of the groups or categories.

This worth thru victim status hierarchical system has been main streamed thru D.I.E. (Diversity, Inclusion and Equity)[8] training/indoctrination.

Thru the creation and enfolding of Intersectionality into the tenets of CRT, the CRT They acquired an enormous constituency.

---

[8] DIE requires at least a booklet on its own but in short: Diversity means no white people, Inclusion means excluding whites, and Equity means participation trophies. DIE has become an international, billion dollar a year industry.

CRT allies are not their "friends"

The CRT They appear to only tolerate their intersectional "allies" as long as they all stay in line, advance the cause and do not challenge the dogma.

Any ally that questions or pushes back in any way will be vilified, shouted down and cancelled (aka #AccountabilityCulture).

Some feminist pushed back against trans women gaining access to women's spaces (shelters/prisons) after some of those trans women sexually assaulting women in those spaces. Those feminists found themselves out of the club.

The Trans community is more valuable to the CRT movement than these "rogue" feminists so those feminists are now TERFs[9] and whether they realize it or not, de facto white.

The LGB Alliance group in the UK is currently being vilified by the CRT faithful for a similar offense.

At the end of the day all of CRT's allies should not forget that regardless of how many checkmarks they have or how important they are made to feel right now; the only people that will be allowed into CRT holy land will be authentic Black.

---

[9] Trans Exclusionary Radical Feminists

Race is the Primary Characteristic of a Human

Never mind Martin Luther King Jr's "...content of their character not the color of their skin..." stuff, CRT only cares about race.

CRT They state that you are either Black or a Racist, that's it, and only CRT They can determine which one you are.

So what exactly does that mean?

Well, either you are an authentic Black or you are a racist.

An authentic Black is an un/under educated[10] black person whose ancestors were slaves in America.

An authentic Black has not benefited from any institution that has been created by systemic racism.

Basically CRT They believe that all Western institutions have been created by systemic racism so all of those institutions are inherently racist and any black person that benefits from any of those institutions will not be "authentic".

Currently CRT They seem to acknowledge other races or racial labels, i.e. POC (People of Color) but this is more than likely a

---

[10] Since educational institutions are all deemed White/racist, a black person that has received a K-12 education or attended university has benefited from systemic racism and is no longer "authentic". These rules obviously do not apply to the CRT They elites.

concession the CRT They have made to advance their movement by (temporarily) allowing non-authentic blacks to join and support them.

Anyone can be declared De facto White
Just because you weren't born white doesn't mean that you aren't White.

The CRT They have the power to declare you de facto White which will remove your previous race/category/identity and make you White (and the enemy). There is no recourse and no being allowed back in the club.

Critical/Correct Think vs. White/Wrong Think
The CRT They believe that critical/correct thinking is subjective[11], race biased, and advances a political agenda.

Whereas wrong/white thinking is objective, neutral and facts based[12].

This tenet is important to understand when attempting to address CRT and its followers. In the minds of the CRT They, feelings trump facts, emotions trump science, someone's

---

[11] Think "your" truth instead of "the" truth.
[12] Their words, not mine.

"personal" truth trumps logic and reason. Someone's "lived experience" is equivalent to divine scripture.

This tenet also enables the CRT They to deny science, reality and re-write history.[13]

There is only one cause for all effects: Racism
In CRT land, if a person "feels" that 2 + 2 = 5, then it does.

If you disagree, you are a racist.

Likewise, if a CRT believer states that the sun will rise in the west on the following day and it doesn't.

That's racism.

If an unqualified CRT believer applies for a job and doesn't get it.

That's because of racism.

And if an unqualified CRT believer applies for a job and **does** get it.

You guessed it, that is also because of racism.

---

[13] #1619 Project

CRT advocates are neo-Marxists

Marxism[14] in a nutshell: no personal belonging, the ruling class owns everything and distributes resources in an "equitable" manner[15]. Marxists strive for the creation of a communist utopia thru a violent socialist revolution.

The CRT They of course will be the new ruling class that will own everything and they will determine who is worthy and who is not.

FYI, White and de facto White will not be allowed.

CRT has 2 Objectives

Deconstruct (destroy) all White Institutions

The CRT They believe that every principle and ideal that America was built upon is White and systemically racist. So anything that is American is inherently White and inherently racist.

The CRT They further believe that the only way forward is to deconstruct (destroy) everything that is inherently White/racist.

---

[14] For a much deeper explanation of Marxism (and several other relevant topics) check out Ryan Chapman's YouTube channel
[15] See Venezuela

In short, America, the Constitution, American culture, capitalism, Christianity, and the West all must be deconstructed.

The CRT they seek to deconstruct the legal and justice system, our financial systems, our schools and universities, our mores and norms and anything that contributes to our functioning society.

The CRT They are not proposing modifications to existing structures. They seek the complete destruction of America so that a non-racist society can be built on its ashes.

Re-Segregation of America

A significant milestone in their quest is the re-introduction of segregation.

We have already seen this happening in our elementary schools.

Our children are being separated by race and black children can only be taught by black teachers.

Recently construction of a "woke" self-sustaining city was proposed that would be an example of our future, and you guessed it, no White is allowed.

Abolish White

The CRT They have made it perfectly clear, as long as White is allowed to exist there can be no country, system or institution that is free of White's oppression and tyranny.

As long as White exists, racism exists.

To the best of my knowledge, I do not believe the CRT They have called for the deaths of all white people but I do believe there is at least footage of CRT "activists" calling for the death of particular white people.

The CRT They's objectives are to be accomplished thru a violent socialist revolution, ideally resulting in the complete destruction of America so that a new non-racist black nation can be built upon its ashes.

A close second place end goal is for a black sovereign nation to be carved out of America and paid for thru reparations and the spoils of war.

Part 2: What we can do about it

This is not a fight, we are all Americans
As much as the CRT They want to make this a culture war and divide us by race, we cannot let them.

This is not a war and we are all the same race, the human race.

Love, respect, compassion, acceptance and understanding.

We are all Americans and remember, diversity, true diversity is our strength.

The great melting pot that is America, all who have come have contributed to what it means to be an American. Our shared differences define us as much as what we have in common.

There is no such thing as Cultural Appropriation
The adoption and incorporation of aspects of all of the people's cultures that have come to America thru our history has played a major role in American culture being one of the most creative, innovative and magnificent cultures in the history of human kind.

Celebrating our differences makes us beautiful. Celebrating what we share makes us Americans.

Reject CRT wherever you encounter it
Do not remain silent.

Denounce CRT, wokism, white fragility, white guilt, gender identity politics, socialism, communism, Marxism, fascism and any of the "neo" flavors of those ideologies/religions whenever and wherever they are forced upon you.

Equality not Equity
Equality of opportunity is the American promise. Equity of outcome is participation trophies. No one wants to see me in the Olympics. Equality means I can try out. Equity means I'm on the team.

Let go of the past
It is critical that we teach our shared history so we do not repeat our mistakes.

It is not critical or relevant to teach a re-envisioned "history" of myth and fantasy to advance an agenda[16].

The history that we teach our children should not be whitewashed or blackwashed[17]. It should be a celebration of the

---

[16] #1619 Project
[17] Thomas Sowell is an author and a black history scholar, well worth looking up

great American experiment with full disclosure of any and all of the times that we fell short or didn't get it right.

History without context is propaganda. The only agenda that should be involved is to educate.

Teaching history thru a modern day "filter" of mores and norms is irresponsible at best and more than likely straight up disingenuous[18].

Focus on the now and the future, on coming together as a people and as a country to address our very real and very current challenges.

Focus on engaging others with good faith, compassion and acceptance[19].

Disagreeing is a good thing.

Shouting down, attempting to cancel or assaulting those who disagree with you is not.

Do not go looking for hate, you **will** find it.

---

[18] See the previous statement about propaganda
[19] Acceptance does not mean you agree, it means you accept that others think different than you and that they have every right to do so

Do not get angry
Your anger is all that the CRT They need to label you a racist and then their mob will come for you.

No name calling
"When the debate is lost, slander becomes the tool of the loser."[20]

The constructive discussion ends when "racist", "Nazi", "fascist" or any other "ophobe" insult comes out of your mouth.

If your argument is solely based on the other person being "bad" or "stupid" you probably need to get educated on your own position before engaging in further discussions.

If you cannot control your emotions, best to leave the discussing to those who can.

No Violence
if the time comes for violence, America will already be lost.

---

[20] Apparently, said by no one. Current fact check on this says no verified attribution to Socrates

We must stop the indoctrination of our children

Indoctrinators[21] should be given the opportunity to stop. If they can't/won't they should be replaced.

In the last few months several K-12 teachers have been exposed as CRT indoctrinators, mostly by their own open and self-congratulatory admissions. It was very encouraging that these teachers were relieved of their duties once their intentions, agendas, and curriculums were made public.

CRT, just like any other hate speech/propaganda should be banned from schools.

Know your child's teacher and curriculum. Meet the teacher in person, review your child's school materials.

Visit your child's school and go to their classrooms.

The only flags allowed in schools and classrooms should be the American and state flags.

If the teacher has pictures of mass murdering tyrants[22] on the walls this should be a huge red flag.

Do not let the indoctrination continue.

---

[21] Teachers/professors
[22] Think Stalin or Mao

Reject Segregation

As mentioned previously, we currently have schools in America that are segregating students by race.

I doubt there is a single university that doesn't have all black fraternities and sororities and obviously we have all black colleges and universities.

Segregation divides America and is bad in all forms and all justifications.

Get the Pledge of Allegiance back in our schools and yes, everyone, including the teacher participates. No kneeling or "mostly peaceful protesting" allowed.

And no, there should NOT be 2 national anthems.

Do not Pay for the Revolution

Do not support organizations or businesses that support CRT overtly or passively.

I get it, this is harder than it sounds.

Almost every corporation has bent the knee to the CRT They and woke "accountability" mobs. Any company that does not comply risks boycotts, protests and in some cases smashed windows, looting and/or fire bombing.

Any business that resists should get your support and your business.

You can speak with your money.

You can also ask to speak to a manager and explain that due to their business' choice to support hate you are not supporting them. No need to argue, just state your feelings and leave.

Engage your Representatives

The school board, the city council, your state and federal representatives, let them know that the CRT movement is not welcome and that your money and your votes will not support it.

In short, America is worth saving.

God Bless you, God Bless me, God Bless us and

God Bless America.

Made in the USA
Columbia, SC
06 October 2021